Plan It Now!

Quit the Burnout Business and Become a Creative Entrepreneur

By Tracy Durrant

Plan It Now! Quit the Burnout Business and Become a Creative Entrepreneur

Plan your creative business in 10 days - Written by Tracy Durrant

First edition published December 2018

Download the Free Business Model Success Quiz

If you want this book to be personalised for you, this quiz will red-light the parts of your business that you need to work on the most.

www.tracydurrant.com/planitnow1

For print or media interviews with Tracy, please contact info@tracydurrant.com

ISBN Paperback: 9780995548428

ISBN Ebook: 9780995548435

Published by: Tracy Durrant

www.tracydurrant.com

This book is dedicated to you!

You have big dreams.

You're ready to grow your creative business, and bring more joy and abundance into your life.

Introduction

It's time to leave the grind behind

What's the worst-case scenario if you just stop? I asked myself.

This was summer 2011. I waited for an answer while taking in the views of an almost untouched beachfront, inhaling the ocean's air and feeling the warmth of the white sands in between my toes. For the first time in years, I was giving myself an opportunity to breathe, to think, to reflect and to ask myself the real questions.

I had been led to Portugal, a place I had been reading about for months prior. I was drawn to learn more about the history of the Moors. But what I had thought would be a great opportunity to relax and explore the country's past, became an altogether different mission. I had no awareness of how that trip would change the course of my life.

For seven years, I'd been dodging the 9-5, but being pulled in five different directions by my business hadn't been the plan. I'd chosen this life, yet I felt trapped. A creative entrepreneur who was feeling neither creative nor entrepreneurial. Life was stressful and I wasn't sure who I could turn to for practical, emotional and spiritual support. I had multiple interests, was feeling overwhelmed and was struggling to make sense of it all.

At that time, though, I didn't understand what a business coach could do to help me, not only navigate through the practicalities of launching, growing and building my business, but the emotional aspects, such as self-doubt, fear, procrastination, overwhelm, the inner critic and tools to help me gain clarity.

Instead, three or four days a week, I was contracting as a PR executive at an agency for consumer, music and fashion brands. On the other days (or sometimes on the same days making use of my evenings and weekends), I worked part time in retail and as a live events promoter for contemporary popular music artists and festivals. And I ran and managed my own PR and events company during all the other hours I could find, whether that was on lunch breaks or on my commute to work.

Work and life were just not balancing up... Doing everything myself, never taking a break, not thinking of my own wellbeing, this was the norm. Worst of all, I lived by the myth that the harder I worked, the more money I would bring in; being 'too busy' became my mantra. I repeated it whenever I had an invitation to go out and enjoy myself. Yet I always made time to pile additional work events onto my plate, anything that looked like an opportunity: networking events in the morning and evening, a 4-hour shift at a music venue. The idea was I could be well-positioned to network at a music venue, but I didn't actually have the time to connect well with anyone. Yep, I was 'too busy'.

I would hold on tight to my money as if I would never make another penny. I only spent on business-related expenses, never considering that investing in my own self-care, beautiful experiences, events, or places I would like to go 'just because' was worth the money. It must have seemed like I was rolling in it because I was associated with big brands, either running my own events or attending concerts and celebrity birthdays, partying with artists one night, then selling their CDs the next day. My life was full of beautiful contradictions.

While working in the PR firm, I'd go from organising photoshoots to contacting magazines, going to awards events to ensuring that the right celebrities would be in attendance for product launches. I saw how companies like MTV, shows like BBC's Children In Need, drinks companies like Disaronno rum and clothing companies like Puma managed their media relations, understanding how celebrity placements really worked, and lending my voice and skills to making things happen.

I was not long out of university, but I've always felt that the real education happens when you're out 'doing the work', so I chose to work for others while leading my own projects head first. This meant I wasn't just working in agencies; I took everything I had learned studying PR, live events management and music technology, and applied the theory and experience to my own start-ups. I would host a monthly music and fashion event, booking artists and DJs, collaborating with venues, contacting local press, tweeting every day and managing a small team of creatives. Doing freelance work with aspiring music artists and designers through my PR and events business, while working for one of the largest live music companies in the world on the side. Bearing the responsibility of good PR with local businesses. Ensuring the venues and festivals in London were well attended. Being paid to promote music. All this added up to a dream job, with benefits including complimentary entry to some of my favourite artists at the time, Erykah Badu, Raphael Saadiq, J Cole and many more. On top of it all, I worked in retail part time selling headphones, CDs and DVDs. Not to mention song-writing and designing my own clothing brand. My days and weeks had no structure, except keeping busy.

I learned so much about business and myself in that phase of my life, but my business didn't quite make sense.

Funnily enough, back then, I used a business plan. It was big and bulky and had all the pages outlined as suggested in most popular business books: business key objectives, skills and experience, target customers, research, competition, sales projections, operational plan, marketing plan, plus all the financial projections, including cash flow forecasts and break-even charts. I became a whizz at Excel and understood how to research and document exactly how I would start and grow my business, whether I pursued the PR and events boutique or my clothing brand.

Maybe you can relate. Maybe you too have business plans way out of proportion to your actual enterprise or pages and pages of planning leaving you no time for what you're really great at, the fun stuff, or a life outside your business

YOU DON'T NEED ALL THAT. YOU CAN PLAN A BUSINESS ON A PAGE.

It can be simple and creative. And this book will show you how. Plan It Now! is not about reading.

It's about doing. That's why you'll have practical worksheets at the end of each section coaching you through a method of business planning that I wish I'd known back in 2011, back when I decided to quit the busyness... and focus on carving out the business I had always dreamed of running.

The clear decision that arrived in my mind as I waited on that Portugal beach changed everything. I wanted to get back in control of my life so that my business worked for me, not the other way around. Landing back in London, I stared down the 10 themes in the next 10 chapters. And in 10 days, life looked unrecognisable and oh-so much better.

Now business unfolds naturally because I'm clear about what I want.

I organise my weeks around what I desire, so I can spend time away from work worry-free. I attract the right clients. My time is mine. This isn't about having a million dollars. It's about making a decision to live with joy. I see people making more money and still not taking control of their life. They aren't getting the money or fulfilment they want out of their business or life, because they haven't made the decision. They end up having their business run them rather than the other way around. They don't understand that they're deserving of a joyful abundant life.

On one of the hottest days of the summer in 2018, I sat on a restaurant roof terrace at one of the trendiest members-only clubs for creative entrepreneurs with my friend having lunch.

It was a weekday. I was in no rush to finish my meal. And I made the decision to stay there for the day to enjoy beautiful conversations and connect with other creatives living in the flow.

We shared stories of how far we'd come, of how not working in the middle of the week would have been unthinkable not so long ago, but now we have none of that guilt, none of that 'I should be doing something more to grow my business'. The struggle had lifted because I'd clarified what was important. I'd decided to make 'joy, ease and flow' my mission and give up my struggle story.

Knowing I've got a system in place and a team to support me that I trust. Understanding that taking a break from the office, leaving the laptop at home and having my phone on silent is perfectly okay. This is what it means to be present, and that is a real gift to myself and others.

Each floor of the building was filled with creatives who have chosen to live a life they love. There are happy faces all round, a fragrance of inspiring conversations in the air, people relaxing in the pool, having dinner, masterminding in groups, others sipping a drink alone on their laptops.

Looking out, I took in the hustle and bustle of London, creatives, entrepreneurs, ex-9-5ers who weren't falling for the trap anymore, not trading their most valuable gift of time for busyness.

Nobody appeared in a rush to be anywhere, not because they were less important or profitable than stressed-out busy people, but because they'd prioritised fulfilment over filling their every waking hour. While everyone had their own agenda, this club facilitated people to naturally build great relationships from an authentic place. It was not the environment to fish for clients. It was not about feast or famine. This was about creative entrepreneurship. And it was exactly where I wanted to be.

Now I choose who I want to work with and I prioritise myself. I'm no longer chasing calls and opportunities. More synchronicities arise. Life falls into place. I'm at peace with the flow of the business. The best part is my business is more profitable than ever.

I can hear your resistance rising, but if you think about it, more flow makes perfect business sense...

And it's closer than you think.

You just need to claim it for yourself.

And that's why we're here. To help you claim it. To allow it to happen. This plan will help you create the framework. Then the shift will follow as a result of clarity and decisions.

Do the worksheets. Transfer them to the one-page plan. These simple 10 steps will initiate that control over your business.

This book isn't just about business.

Getting this level of clarity and developing the skills outlined in this book will serve you not only in your business, but also in your life. It creates balance. With balance, you're happier healthier and more successful. That's what I want for you. A healthy abundant life. And I want you to want this for yourself too, because the alternative serves no one.

I'm location-free. I have time to do what I want with who I want. I'm happier, healthier, and making better income. From Portugal, it would take another five years to harness the true power of the one-page business plan. It will take you 10 days. I hope you find this as useful as I did.

Why did you pick up this book?

You've picked up this book because you're ready to commit your creative ideas to paper. You want a plan and you're not looking to spend the next six months getting the basics down. Or you may have run your business for a while and identified a few gaps, maybe in your marketing, maybe the numbers are not adding up, maybe your distribution is not supporting you.

Why write a one-page plan?

At the end of each section of this book, questions will guide you to complete the related block on your Creative Business Model Map.

Each day, you will see which block on your Map corresponds with the answers you have just given.

All you need to do is summarise your answer onto a sticky note and stick it onto your Map.

Go to www.tracydurrant.com/mymap to download your one-page plan AKA the Creative Business Model Map.

Why it's important to commit your ideas to paper and make a plan.

1. **Reduce distractions:** If you have no strategy, you may find yourself getting distracted, unsure if a new idea, opportunity or partnership is something you should say yes or no to. If you have a plan, you'll be able to see if and how the 'new idea' fits in. As creatives, it's easy for us to get distracted by 'shiny objects'. I know I've done this many times when I didn't have a plan. Remember, just because you can it doesn't mean you should.

2. **Build confidence:** When you lack confidence, it's hard to bring others on board, but you'll need to create a team to grow your business. If you're going to bring others on board, you need to be clear about why you're bringing them on board. A plan will help you describe your business with confidence.

3. **Get structure:** Writing a plan will prevent you from creating an idea, then creating another and another, before working out what area of your business needs support. It allows you to address each area in order of priority, instead of creating idea after idea without any direction or logic.

4. **Understand your business:** Doing a business plan will help you understand what areas are being taken care of, where you need to hire people, where you're doing really well, and what areas could use some help. Plus, you'll have an overview of how your entire business works.

5. **Embrace creative freedom:** This is my favourite reason. Having a plan gives you space to be creative. Yes, having structure allows your creativity to flourish as it gives you the breathing space needed for inspiration to come to you. It's much easier to discover a way to be creative within bitesize sections of your business, rather than staring at the whole business and trying to find new approaches.

Traditional business planning vs the Creative Business Model Map

A traditional business plan can send many aspiring and well-tuned business owners into a panic.

Writing a business plan can feel like a lengthy process of dragging out all the details and ideas from your head onto paper as a way to prove that they will be financially viable, and worthy of investment and time.

Business plans are amazing for teasing out details but often leave business owners feeling disconnected, exhausted and sometimes uninspired. Why? Because a business plan is so much about what your business is and needs to do, as opposed to who you and your business desire to be.

Let's shift from the space of doing and look closer at being. I was introduced to the distinct difference between writing a business plan and the thinking it takes to run a business by a mentor I met in 2008. Peter had set up an award and centre for aspiring entrepreneurs to get the support they needed to start their business. I won this award. The prize? An office space and mentoring.

Peter gave me two valuable pieces of information when I was starting out. First, speak to someone new about your business every day. And second, take the time to do business planning.

I was confused. I thought I'd done that. In order to win the award, I'd submitted a lengthy business plan. He explained that the plan had little to do with running my business. "Now write a business plan that includes how you will really work your plan", he said. The penny dropped. While the business plan had been valuable in getting through the red tape, that kind of plan was not going to help me with the practicalities of running my business.

Years later, following complete burnout from doing too much, I had another realisation. Simplifying and understanding what I want my business to feel like and how I want to be within that business was just as important as all the practical action steps I outlined.

This became the next iteration of simple, creative, one-page business planning.

You can design your business and life however you want. You hold the paintbrush and decide on the colours that bring your business and life together. When planning your business, be sure to work out exactly how you want to be, what you want to do and what you'd like to have as a result of sharing your gift with the world.

Plan It Now! is about just that. Supporting you to consider the core blocks of your business while putting your needs first.

Getting Started

"With every experience, you alone are painting your own canvas, thought by thought, choice by choice." ~ Oprah Winfrey, Entrepreneur, Producer and Philanthropist

By the time you finish this book, your business plan will be mapped out. It'll be easy for you to see how all the pieces come together so you can focus on growing your successful business.

How to use this book

Go through the book step by step, put some relaxing music on, burn a candle or some incense, make yourself a nice cup of tea, write down the answers that come to mind and enjoy the process of imagining your business into being.

Creating a business and life that excites you every day includes enjoying the process, not spending all your time thinking about the results you want. Those results will come, but you must appreciate the journey too.

Tools

Throughout this book, you'll see worksheets to help you dive deep into the questions. Then you put it all together on your Creative Business Model Map at page 119. If you prefer a printable version, go to www.tracydurrant.com/mymap to download your own copy of the one-page plan.

Don't overthink it!

The worksheets at the end of each section are there to support you in getting the answers you'll need to write onto your sticky notes. You'll be asked to set your timer for 10 or 20 minutes each time, so you can get straight to the point. Often our best ideas come out first, so this process will support you in trusting your instincts and following your intuition.

Ideally, you'll have fun planning your business, so print your Creative Business Model Map and pin it on your wall or desk. Use sticky notes, colourful pens. Then add your answers for each section in short form. Watch the building blocks of your business come together. Block by block. Until you have the full picture.

So let's do this!

Start by exploring where you are with your current business idea.

Set your timer for 20 minutes and answer the following questions:

Business Name/Idea:

_____

What dream or vision do you have for yourself and your business?

_____

_____

_____

What does your business look like today and how would you like it to look in 12 months' time?

_____

_____

_____

What would be your most desired outcome from this book?

_____

_____

_____

Do your clients/customers provide you with enough income to grow your business and lifestyle? Explain why or why not.

_____

_____

_____

Day 1

Mission and Vision: Where do you want to go?

"If you don't have a vision you're going to be stuck in what you know. And the only thing you know is what you've already seen." ~ Iyanla Vanzant, Lawyer, Speaker, Author

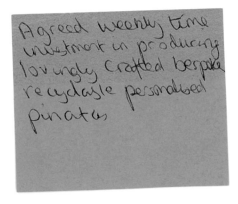

Agreed weekly time investment in producing lovingly crafted bespoke recyclable personalised pinatas

Vision

Having a vision keeps you going while riding the rollercoaster of your business. The vision is where you're heading, the destination of your business, the dream you'd like to end up with, but it's so much more than that. As creative entrepreneurs, often we have a powerful vision for how our work will impact the lives of the people we serve, while ignoring this critical part: who do we need to become to make that vision a reality?

So many of us write ourselves out of our business vision. And when we get stuck in business, it's usually for this reason. We are the missing piece. It's no wonder so many of us reach exhaustion or feel tired of being in business for ourselves; often, we have never been factored in.

Your vision should include who you'd like to be in your business. What would you like to have and what you see yourself doing? What is the dream?

The vision of where you fit into the picture must be so clear that you could close your eyes and step into it. It's important to see what's possible for you and add the juicy details, if not in words at least in your mind. What is your life going to be like? How can you write a vision that works for you, not the other way around?

Mission

Your mission refers to the actions or steps you take. This is more practical than the vision, which looks to the future. It's based in the now, on, specific activities you're doing right now. It's action based.

A fashion designer's mission could be making beautiful clothes for work-from-home entrepreneurs. All the to-dos could include where and how the clothes are produced.

Yet her vision would be that she sees her clothes being sold in Paris, New York and London in exclusive boutiques. Or that her clothing line reaches number one as the go-to store for women entrepreneurs.

Going deeper into the vision, she may see herself designing her collection in the sunshine while outsourcing all the major parts of the business to a team that she loves interacting with once a week on Skype. She may love that once a quarter she can take her entire team on a tropical retreat to mastermind and recharge.

Now let's write yours, making the vision and mission statements as succinct as possible.

Tips for writing your Vision and Mission Statements

1. Make them short and easy to remember
2. Use simple language. Drop any jargon, lingo or business/industry-specific talk.
3. Focus on words that inspire you. Words that describe a scene. Think about what you want and how you want to feel.

Here are some examples from well-known entrepreneurs:

"To be a teacher. And to be known for inspiring my students to be more than they thought they could be." ~ Oprah Winfrey, Founder of OWN, The Oprah Winfrey Network

"To use my gifts of intelligence, charisma, and serial optimism to cultivate the self-worth and net-worth of women around the world." ~ Amanda Steinberg, Founder of dailyworth.com

"To have fun in [my] journey through life and learn from [my] mistakes." ~ Sir Richard Branson, Founder of The Virgin Group

Write your own Vision and Mission Statements

Use the above personal vision statements for inspiration. These showcase entrepreneurs putting themselves into their vision. While you write your vision and mission statements, please remember to consider where you are in the picture. Add a line or two on that.

Set your timer for 10 minutes and envision your life and business dream:

Write your Vision Statement here. Detail the vision you see for your business.

_____

_____

_____

Set your timer for 10 minutes and get clear on what the mission looks and feels like:

Write your Mission Statement. Describe what you do.

_____

_____

_____

Map it

Do you have two clear statements to describe your vision and mission? Add your Vision and Mission Statements to separate sticky notes and stick to the corresponding section of your Map. Take one more sticky note and add the date to the top.

You've completed your first block. Only nine more to go for a simple creative business plan!

Day 2

Business Models for Abundance

"Information technology is at the core of how you do your business and how your business model itself evolves." ~ Satya Nadella, Business Executive

Business models are more important than ever, because the internet has revolutionised everything! They're so essential should another change come in.

The internet changed the way we do business What's going to impact the way you run your business in two, five or ten years from now? Let's say Blockchain technology shifts the way we do business within the next few years. You'll need to be ready for change and a grasp of your business model is how you do that. Are you ready or will you bury your head and not budge, the same way Blockbuster didn't move when approached by Netflix?

You need to be aware of your business foundation and understand how it could shift. Regardless of whether you build your business on the rock or the sand, change is inevitable. Creating this Map is about being ready for growth now and embracing the future too.

New opportunities sprout up anywhere and everywhere. If you have any sort of talent, there's a business model for it. It's essential to familiarise yourself with exactly how your business model works so that you make money, and are flexible and aware enough to shift with this ever-changing landscape.

Your Business Model Map forms the foundation to your business. By having a business model, you don't only get to see how all the different parts of your business work together on one page, but you also have a quick and easy way to visualise change. Simply by removing a sticky note and replacing it with something else. This helps you to stay in flow.

What is a Business Model?

A business model speaks to the plan implemented by a company to generate revenue and make a profit from operations. The model includes the components and functions of the business as well as the revenue it brings in and expenses it incurs. Having a model mapped out for you will help you see what may work in your situation and give you flexibility to shift when needed.

Example of a product-based business model

With the internet creating opportunities for new business models to emerge, you only need to browse the range of apps available on your phone to witness the potential. In this section, we'll summarise the framework of a product-based business model and how technology has impacted it.

There are hundreds of models out there, but I've chosen to focus on this example as it demonstrates how technology has impacted various aspects of the business from reaching customer, production and delivery. Much can be learned from looking at this model and some of the methods can be applied to a service-based business model.

How Product-Based Businesses Have Changed

One word: dropshipping!

Let me explain what this new delivery process means for product-based businesses.

Not so long ago, if you had an idea for a T-shirt business, a typical model would include finding or creating the designs, sourcing T-shirt and printers, then ordering your items to be printed. Most places would require you to meet a minimum order due to set-up costs, meaning you'd need to invest in samples up-front at a premium.

When I was making and selling T-shirts, I paid the initial set-up fee per design based on how many colours featured (common when screen printing). This fee was non-negotiable. I'd need to order my stock, store it at home, then sell the T-shirts. On three occasions, I was involved in T-shirt start-ups; on all three occasions, I tested the market at festivals, events and the popular Camden Market in London.

Today with the availability of digital printing and dropshipping, you can test your ideas and designs with your dream customers from home by investing little to no money at all, especially if you have the design skills and know how to create a website or get up and running on Wordpress or Squarespace, you can start sharing content to attract your dream customers right away.

Sites like Facebook, Twitter, Instagram and a whole host of others make it easier every day to transform your ideas into engaging content from videos, live video & pictures. We have the ability to broadcast our ideas instantly at our fingertips which is great for a product-based business to establish demand prior to making large investments.

Digital printing means printers don't need to charge per colour like they did with screen printing. Dropshipping can mean the item is only made when an order has been placed, saving you up-front costs.

There are many tools available to allow you to create designs, upload them to dropshipping sites, and use their plugins with your website to help you start selling products internationally within an hour of coming up with the concept.

In addition, companies like Amazon offer dropshipping services that take care of inventory and product delivery. For example, let's say you want to sell paper planners. Maybe you import the stock from a different country but don't have storage space to hold inventory until you receive orders. You could use Amazon's dropshipping service to take care of packaging and delivery when customers order your products.

Modern technology also allows online businesses to add automation, automate promotional offers via email, send out invoices, abandoned shopping basket reminders, systems to help save time by not needing to repeat work, making the most out of your input and systemising the work so you can focus on what you love. All these tools can help make growing your business more fun allowing you to really grow a business around your own personal needs, desires and your family life.

This example shows how technology has influenced the product-based business model, from start-up costs, running costs, marketing methods (as you can promote online and establish demand before going to print) as well as making use of various tools to build and maintain relationships,

No matter what type of business you have or decide to create, it's important to be aware of the changes that happen around you, and have a system that allows you to identify and implement changes if need be.

There are many more business models out there. Let's take a look at yours and how to make it adaptable in case of shifts in your industry.

What's been happening in your industry?

It's time to take a glimpse at your business - past, present and future. You've read how technology has impacted three types of businesses. What about your industry.

These questions help you complete your Creative Business Model Map, as you may identify opportunities and risks. These answers won't be added to the Map, but this information may be relevant in the future.

Set your timer for 20 minutes and answer the following three questions:

What did your industry look like in the past?

_____

_____

_____

What does your industry look like now?

_____

_____

_____

What may the future hold for your industry and why?

_____

_____

_____

Day 3

Align with Your Dream Customer

"Don't find customers for your products; find products for your customers." ~ Seth Godin, Marketing Specialist and Author

By now, I'm sure you have an idea of who your customers are, so this is about looking closer at your dream niche and customers, developing an understanding for why they would love to purchase from you.

I've seen countless entrepreneurs stress out when trying to niche down and limit themselves to one dream customer to reach. In reality, businesses serve multiple customers in different ways, at different levels, at different price points, at different times.

While I understand it's important to have a niche, once you discover how to work that area well, you may want to explore how to niche across. To niche across would be to expand your niche offering and look at how and what you offer across a wider audience, multiple audiences or the same customer at different stages (see points 1 and 2 below).

Why limit yourself to one specific ideal customer when you can have more? Expanding your business to serve multiple audiences and aligning your product with the specific customer group means more people get to benefit from the gift of your service. Once you know who your customers are, you're likely to spot customer segments, maybe some that were always there but you paid little attention to while focusing on that single ideal customer.

Customer segments are key groups of customers with slightly different characteristics:

1. **They come to your business at different stages in their development for the service you offer.** For example, if you offer a coaching service, one client segment may only be ready to start their journey with you through your books, so the entry level could be a book. The next level may look like an online program. A level up from there may be one-to-one coaching or retreats. You share the same coaching information and operate in the same niche, but the service, level of access and price point are different depending on the type of customer.

2. **They purchase your product for different reasons.** If you have a product, you may have customers who love the off-the-shelf offering. You may also have customers who will always go for the bespoke option. Think of coffee shops. Some people go because they love gourmet coffee. They explore the coffee regions, flavours and new concoctions. Others may be business

owners coming for regular hours and a quiet comfortable peaceful place to work.

Knowing who your customer groups are and what they desire can help you get creative with how you show up and serve them. This helps position you as the 'go-to' in your industry.

Understanding the reasons your customers come to you and recognising that they all have different needs (even though it may appear like they want the same thing) will open doors for you to have fun with tailor-made services or products that speak to their soul and unlock exciting ways of attracting money into your business.

Once you really know who you're here for, you can serve them in profound and creative ways.

Who wants coffee?

Let's take a more detailed look at customer segments using our coffee house example.

Coffee Lovers

These customers come because they love coffee. How can a coffee shop business get creative knowing this information? By providing coffee from different parts of the world, educating their customers about coffee, displaying knowledge about the regions on the wall, creating experiences where coffee drinkers can meet other like-minded coffee connoisseurs, making decorative cups and impressive designs from the coffee foam, jazzing up the added extras and much more.

Business Owner

Need to stay caffeinated? You aren't alone. This kind of customer just can't stand working at home; maybe it's too noisy, maybe there are too many distractions, maybe they want to block certain hours of work each day to get their head into a project, maybe they don't trust themselves with the fridge and always end up eating way too much or watching TV. This customer may not even like coffee, so the shop owner could diversify the range of hot and cold drinks, with and without caffeine.

Coffee shops that want to attract the business owner customer segment will provide tables large enough for a laptop and diary, daily newspapers so customers can keep updated with current affairs, comfy chairs that keep them there all day and free WiFi. The longer the customer stays, the more drinks and food they'll consume!

Group Work

Then you have students, who are there because they need space. For students, coffee shops can offer a range of facilities, such as large conference tables or private meeting rooms, providing them plenty of space for project planning.

Down memory lane...

Reflecting on the early 2000s, if you wanted to access the internet in London while away from home (if you were lucky enough to have internet at home), you'd have to go to internet cafes. Few phones had internet. And if they did, it would be too slow to be useful. Certain websites just wouldn't work at all.

In a few short years, coffee shops earned their place on every high street, not only offering free WiFi in most cases, but also comfort and refreshments. Knowing that many people now carry a computer or smartphone (just as powerful these days), all coffee shops need to do is provide the space. The customers take care of the rest.

Some coffee shops would have spotted a trend in the way customers want to buy and experience drinking coffee and many shops in the UK have adapted their business model from simply providing a cup of coffee as an alternative to a cup of tea to rebranding their entire shops, introducing multiple take away cup sizes and making the environment a place for multiple customer segments to enjoy sitting in or taking away their drink.

In the early 2000s, it's possible that business development teams and marketing departments would have identified that the internet was going to be at the heart of all communication across generations and that there was a growing trend of drinking coffee. There are a number of ways marketing departments can spot trends: from pop culture (TV shows of the time included Friends where the characters always met at a coffee shop) to business reports (Keynotes, Mintel or other specific bodies that monitor consumer behaviour).

Some companies who keep an eye on trends would have identified several customer segments and have had an idea of how to provide value to each group, not only for that point in time, but also in years to come. So, you see how taking time to plan your business supports you not only now but also in years to come.

It's amazing how the coffee industry is growing through its creativity. There's so much we can learn just from visiting coffee shops. It's also a great place to learn to identify your customer groups. Coffee shops do it well. Look at your audience now and ask yourself: what fun can I have making money and serving these people?

Aligning with your dream customers is a two-step process, where you first **define** your customer groups, then **decide** exactly what you can do to provide value to them.

Defining Your Customer Groups

Now over to you!

Set your timer for 20 minutes, and read and answer the questions below.

Once you're done, write your customer groups and the value you'll bring them onto sticky notes and add to your Map.

Who are the three core customer groups you enjoy serving? (If you only serve one type of customer, think about the different products they may need from you at different stages of their journey.)

The coffee shop example has three different types of customers. Let's say you work with entrepreneurs. That customer may progress through various stages, starting in one group (such as a start-up), then going on to a stage of stability, then desiring next level success. Products and services that served them as a start-up will be completely different to the next-level-success stage.

Consider this when exploring your three customer groups if it doesn't seem obvious at first.

1.

2.

3.

Map it!

Are you clear who your three core customer segments are? Write each group clearly on separate sticky notes and put them under the customer groups section on your Map.

Add them by order of priority in terms of who you want to focus on, where they come in the customer journey, or the amount of revenue each group brings in. Do what works for you.

Aligning with your customers

Let's spend some time exploring how you are providing and can offer value to each of your customer groups. What can you do to really serve your customers and provide real solutions to the challenges they face?

Remember to include services that you enjoy delivering and that align with your customers. Look at each group on the Map and ask the following questions:

What is your customer's main pain point?

What do you offer that relieves this pain point for them?

What do you offer that's irresistible?

_____

_____

_____

What is it about your service that your customers find valuable?

_____

_____

_____

What could you do to provide more of that value?

_____

_____

_____

Map it!

Peel off three sticky notes and add at least three ways you can align with your customers by catering to the needs of each group. Stick next to each customer segment that you've already added on the Map, under the header 'Aligning With Customers'.

Congratulations! You've completed the first three building blocks of your creative business model canvas! Do something to celebrate, even if it's just taking a break to make yourself a cup of tea.

Day 4

Creating Real Connections with Customers

"I've learned that people will forget what you said, people will forget what you did, but people will never forget how you made them feel." ~ Maya Angelou, Author and Poet

In this day and age, there's no reason to disconnect from customers or fail to nurture relationships with people who are excited to hear from you. It has never been easier. And yet it can be easy to fall into a trap of vanity metrics, a need to see large numbers of followers before engaging or feeling like the amount of people interested isn't enough. Your business growth will depend on your ability to identify, establish and nurture relationships, sometimes blending online and offline activities. It's time to open up and connect to your people?

Business is personal. As with all personal relationships, there's an element of vulnerability. Are you ready to share your heart, your values, your truth with your customers so they feel comfortable sharing with you?

Static automated content has its place as a reminder to your audience that you exist, but does little in connecting you with the people you serve. Instead, we do business with people we know, like and trust. I'm sure you've heard this before, but what does it really mean?

In this chapter, you'll get clear on what methods of connection are exciting for you when it comes to building relationships with your customers and establishing communication methods that work for your community.

Included in this, we'll look at the frequency of communication that will keep them inspired and connected with your message and the platform or method you like to use. The internet has expanded the ways we connect, be it email, live streaming, daily 15-second snippets of video content, hosting your own show, video calls. Maybe it's Instagram where you build relationships. Perhaps you love, love, love engaging with your customers over the phone? Offline tools to establish loyalty shouldn't be overlooked. Could hosting a regular local event be the catalyst to strengthening ties between you and the people you serve?

Once you establish the communication method that works for you, building and maintaining relationships will be easy and fun. And, of course... creative.

How coffee shop chains build relationships

Let's take another look at our coffee shop example. Here are a number of ideas that demonstrate how coffee shops encourage loyalty.

Loyalty Cards

Front of mind, most coffee shops have a loyalty card scheme along the lines of: buy 9 drinks, get the 10th free. This may be a stamp system, where you present a card and get it stamped each time you go to store, or an app, as many large coffee shop chains have.

The introduction of loyalty cards into coffee shops is a simple but effective way to establish a long-term relationship between the coffee drinker and their company. If you have already invested in a few coffees from that particular coffee shop and know that you'll receive a reward if you buy a few more, the incentive keeps you coming back.

A Loyalty App

When you sign up to a loyalty card app, the company not only gets your email address, which means they can continue to build a relationship with you via your inbox, but they can share insider knowledge like new products or events to see what interests you.

When considering how to connect with your customers, look at how they like to communicate. While most people have a mobile phone, the introduction of a loyalty app is for the more tech-savvy generations, who are more likely to pull out an app than keep a stamp card in their wallet. It comes back to knowing your customer (Please glance at Day 3 for further clarity on aligning with your dream customer).

Social Media Engagement

The rise of the selfie amongst millennials has seen an increase of coffee inspired social media content, something that many coffee shops have tapped into. A popular coffee shop chain has been featured in so many social media posts, that the act of picking up a coffee at their chain and photographing it for Instagram has positioned this coffee shop as a lifestyle brand.

Knowing how Instagramable coffee-related social media posts can be, a popular coffee brand has created competitions where you can do your own designs on the cups and share on social media. The coffee cup photo has become a work of art. Don't believe me? Pull out Instagram and search #coffeecup to see how popular it is.

Those are just three examples of how a coffee shop could build relationships with its customers, from loyalty cards to apps, newsletters and social media competitions. Since all of these methods could appeal to different demographics, take a moment to consider which would best suit the people connecting with you, as well as your own preferences.

How to build relationships with your customers

Let's explore different types of customer relationships. While it's unlikely all will apply to your business, take notes throughout and start thinking about how you'd love to connect with your customers and whether you'd like to implement any of these ideas.

1. **Personal assistance**: Some examples include customer services, call centres, websites where you provide live help, or email offering personal assistance to your customers.

2. **Self-service**: You'll have no direct relationship with your customers. Popular with photo booths, where customers put a coin into the slot, wait for the flash, then get their photo in minutes. Self-service also happens in some retail outlets, where customers use a self-checkout.

3. **Dedicated personal assistance**: Private banks are an example of business that would have a dedicated person who manages client accounts. All banking enquiries would go through one person.

4. Another example would be in PR and marketing agencies where customers are assigned a dedicated person to work with, referred to as an account manager.

5. **Automated services:** Automated services include systems that automate the way your customers interact with you, this could be based on previous purchases, areas clicked on or avoided when visiting your website. It can also include email automation through opting into a newsletter, course or free download. Automation can be used as a way of building a relationship with your customers.

6. **Community-building:** You could create groups where customers interact and connect with each other through a shared interest. The shared interest could be your product or service. A well-run group could help you understand the needs of your customers and provide a two-way communication strategy.

7. **Co-creation:** Any platform that asks its users to upload content is building a relationship with its audience through co-creation. YouTube is a great example of this. YouTube provide the platform and the customer provides the content.

Five-minute reflection:

Think about the last product or service you bought. How did that company build know, like and trust with you? Did they build a relationship with you first? Was it in seconds or did it take years?

_____

_____

_____

What did you like and dislike about the way that company communicated with you? What lessons could you take away for your own business?

_____

_____

_____

Creating and building real connections

Your business will thrive in relation to how effectively you create, build and maintain relationships, so let's explore how you're creating and building real connections with your people!

Set your timer for 10 minutes and complete the answers below:

How do you currently stay connected with your existing and potential customers? (For example, I write a weekly newsletter.)

What type of relationship would you like to have with your existing and potential customers?

What would you need to do to make this a reality?

How will you build relationships with your customer? (For example, I would like to build more trust through holding regular events for customers.)

Map it!

Take a sticky note and write what you do, what you wish to create and what you plan to do in the future to strengthen your efforts for 'building connections' with your customers. Stick your note under the 'Creating Real Connection' section.

Day 5

Reveal Your Unique Talents

"Always be a first-rate version of yourself, instead of a second-rate version of somebody else." ~ Judy Garland, Singer and Actress

Make your business unique in every customer segment

Well, praise emoji and high five to you! You're at the halfway mark! This is where it starts to get exciting. In this chapter, we're talking talent.

When was the last time you went to a shop to buy yourself or a loved one a piece of jewellery? Once you decided on the piece, the sales assistant usually asks what type of box you'd like. The jewellery is already beautiful, but they know that if this is a gift, placing it inside the box adds magic. It provides a few seconds of anticipation. The receiver will wonder, what is it? Maybe a ring?. Receiving a beautiful piece of jewellery in a plastic bag with the tag still on doesn't provide the same appeal as being presented in a beautiful box, right?

What you have to offer is of high value. What you're bringing to the table must touch the souls of your customers and impact their lives. So exploring how you will share and present your gift to them is just as important as the gift itself. Create an experience for them that's so memorable they tell others. How you distribute your product or service is the difference between a 5-star review or being blocked across the networks.

Examples of how businesses shine

Let's expand your view of sharing your work with your personal signature and special touch.

Coffee shop

What could you do as a coffee shop owner to beam brightly and stand apart from the crowd?

First, they'd continue to refer back to the blocks of their Map and reflect on their customer groups and how they plan to bring value. The owner would then need to think about their part within their business and how they wanted their staff to shine in their role.

From here, a coffee shop could reveal its uniqueness to its customers creatively by: having a unique way of serving drinks, quirky cup design, taking care to learn customers' names or singing songs to customers on special occasions.

Next time you're at a restaurant, pay attention to what establishments are doing that you love and what was missing from your experience. Great ideas often come from outside your industry.

Advertising agency

While an advertising agency may distribute their service via adverts on bus stops, billboards, TV, magazines and/or social media, in discovering who they want to serve, they may find one avenue is best for their customers. Let's say they opt for social media advertising; that in itself could include so much: Facebook, YouTube, Twitter, Instagram, Google Ads to name a handful. If this was the chosen route, serving customers would have to get more specialised than simply choosing a platform.

Ideas here include: providing more visual reports to show progress of their delivery, offering a VIP service to clients who are new to social media advertising or including additional offerings like support with applying for Trade Marks, or connecting customers with companies that can support them with other aspects of marketing or design so their clients can have a more enriched service.

Business and life coaches

As a business or life coach, what could you do that sets you apart from others in the industry, simply by the way you deliver your service?

With so many coaches offering live streaming, videos, podcasts, webinars, books and speaking gigs to reach their dream customers - all amazing ways to offer value - what could you do to add your own signature to your brand?

Successful business owners might say they are what makes them stand apart, but you'll need to dig deep into that one to know what it is that makes you you. If you have a personal brand, you must understand what people love about working with you, then do more of that.

Do you deliver your content in a direct straight-talking manner? Do you make people laugh? Does your brand have no face? Does it hide behind hashtags and quotes?

Take a look at the other building blocks of your Creative Business Model Map and think how you'd like customers to feel as they experience your products. Consider your customers' preferences and also how you'd like to deliver your products and services so they're excited to tell the world! Once you understand who your customers are and how you create value, revealing your brand to them should be an exciting process. Remember to have fun with this.

Exploring the phases of your customer journey

We're going to take a look now at how you reveal your products to your customers from discovery through to after purchasing.

1. **Discovery:** People need to be aware that your product/service exists, what it does, what value it provides and what the benefits are.

2. **Evaluation:** Once your customer/client is aware of what you do, then they may start evaluating if they want to go further. This could include looking for testimonials, reviews, proof that you do what you say you do. For example, let's say you're purchasing a new sofa. You've been made aware of a new sofa that's being sold by a certain company. In the evaluation phase, you may check if the style fits into the room, search for reviews from others who've bought from that company, compare prices across stores or websites. You may even want to try before you buy. This is what your customer goes through with your business too.

3. **Purchase made:** A financial transaction has taken place and the customer/client is now showing a commitment.

4. **Delivery of goods:** This is the stage where you deliver the product or service to the

customer! Here you'd consider the packaging and delivery style.

5. **After sale:** Once the product/service has been delivered, what aftercare do you offer? Do you want to continue the relationship? Would your customers like to be kept updated with future products?

Set your timer for 20 minutes and let's see how you'll reveal your products to your customers:

Do you have ideas on the type of customer relationships you'd like to build?

Do you know how you'll deliver your product to your customers? In-person (one-to-one service, at a shop) or virtually (online calls, email)? Will your product arrive in the post (packaging, home delivery)?

What are your customer phases through to delivery? (What are all the steps from discovery to after sale?)

Complete the answers below then use your discoveries to add to the 'Delivery' box on your Map.

Reveal your products to the world with style

Step closer to the experience you provide for your customers before, during and after they discover your products.

How do you currently let your existing and potential customers know that you exist?

_____

_____

_____

Are you happy with how you raise awareness of your business? If yes, what do you love? If not, why not?

_____

_____

_____

What could you do to improve the way people discover your products?

_____

_____

_____

How do you deliver the goods?

What's unique about your approach?

Map it!

You're a pro at this by now, but I'm gonna keep reminding you until it's done. Pull out your sticky notes and write your key commitments to excel at marketing! Keep it short enough to fit on the note, but long enough to remember your core marketing activities. Add that note under 'Delivery'. And BOOM! More than halfway done!

Day 6

Focus on Your Zone of Genius

"Success doesn't come from what you do occasionally. It comes from what you do consistently." ~ Marie Forleo, Entrepreneur, Writer and Philanthropist

Ever felt guilty for wanting to escape from your business, fearful knowing you trust no-one to pick up the tasks that should have been 'done yesterday' or burnt out, crying, trying and failing to put one foot in front of the other. The feeling can be terrifying, like your entire world is crashing in on you. Overnight, you went from motivated and 'I can do it all' to in a slump and 'I can't get out of bed'.

No-one wants to feel like this yet so many of us get to this place. But why? Why do we end up there?

Meet your new friends Delegation, Automation and Outsource. They live to support you in all the tasks gobbling up your time, so you can focus on the area of your business that brings you most joy, sometimes referred to as your Zone of Genius (A phrase coined by The Big Leap author, Gay Hendricks.)

Your capacity for joy and abundance in your business and life depends on how you hone your leadership skills. While I believe it's important to know how most things work in your business, it's even more critical to understand who the best person is for those tasks. And often that person is not you. And that's okay!

To me, there is no point in being a creative entrepreneur and dreading what you have to do each day! So, this chapter and corresponding block on your Map is where you'll explore what's blissful to you, what puts you solidly in your Zone of Genius, and ways to do more of that while delegating, automating or outsourcing the rest. This is how you create a thriving lifestyle running your business successfully while avoiding burnout.

Overwhelm and loss of inspiration can creep up on us bit by bit, every time we do a task that takes us away from our Zone of Genius. You can avoid burning out by understanding what activities keep your business pumping and what tasks don't, but it's more than that; it's also about what activities warm your heart and make you smile, which tasks make you spend an extra hour in bed, staring at the ceiling. Those are the ones that make you feel tired all of a sudden, that once you've completed them, you regain energy and feel like going for a short jog!

Not all activities contribute to the success of your business. Not all activities are even best for you to do in your business. Taking the time to shine a light on what you're spending time doing, and understanding the clear distinction between working in your business (doing tasks) and working on your business (deciding what tasks are essential for moving forward, like taking time to complete your Creative Business Model Map) will help you catapult your productivity and the quality of work that your team produces.

80/20 Rule

Starting with the 80/20 Rule, which states that 80% of your results come from 20% of your actions, it's important for you as the creative business owner to take a look at what's working in your business. Also referred to as 'The Pareto Principle' and 'The Law of the Vital Few', usually only 20% of your activities or efforts are worth pursuing. Once identified, make a conscious effort to do more of that!

Questions to keep in mind:

- What are your business' most important activities?
- What activities are going to bring you the greatest results?
- What activities in your business are generating the most revenue or clients?
- What key activities allow your business to function?
- What does your business need to do to deliver value?

Key activities, sales and marketing

Sales and marketing cover all activities that your business needs to do to get your products or services in front of the people who are ready to purchase. This could include sales calls, email marketing, networking, social media, advertising or PR.

As a rule, marketing falls under the 20% of actions that provide 80% of results. In fact, it's often the part of a business that people leave until the end or fail to do altogether, but it's what connects your business to the people... and the money.

Keep in mind that the 80/20 rule still applies within marketing, so it's important to review and look at what marketing tasks are bringing you the best results.

Other key activities may include production, operations, training, consulting and so on. Below are more examples of key activities for two types of businesses.

Manufacturing Business

If you have a product-based business, key activities that you may include on your Map are:
- Design
- Pattern-making/template
- Sampling and material sourcing
- Production
- Sales and marketing

Service-Based Business

For a services-based business, key activities may include:
- Training, updating your own skills and knowledge, because change happens all the time
- Knowledge management and information sharing
- Consulting
- Sales and marketing

Key activities at the coffee shop

Coming back to our coffee shop case study, let's elaborate on some of the key activities, so that you can start to identify what's really crucial in your business. Remember, looking outside your industry is essential for stirring those creative juices.

Marketing

Looking at any popular coffee shop chain, aside from the general day-to-day operation, marketing is one key activity. Many coffee shop chains invest highly in marketing, with a view to building relationships with their key customers and marketing to them in a way that is in tune with their values.

Research and development

As most coffee shop chains have their own brand of food and drink, so research and development is important for deciding whether new products should be brought into the stores, working out how that might work, and identifying which products need to go.

Supply chain

Similar to the manufacturing business example earlier in this chapter, a coffee shop chain would need to have a tight system for getting the coffee beans from the field to cup.

What's your Zone of Genius?

If you want to have a business and life you love, you need to spend time on activities that make your cells smile. You can't get that happy feeling while drowning in tasks you were not born to do.

I'm a firm believer that it strengthens your business when you know how everything works on a basic level, but you don't need to do All Of The Things. Come, let's look at the core activities that keep your business alive, then see where your genius sits and what innovative ideas you can get stuck into.

Set your timer for 20 minutes and let's see if you're focused on your Zone of Genius by completing the answers below:

What do you love to do?

_____

_____

_____

What were you put on earth to do?

_____

_____

_____

Why is this important?

_____

_____

_____

How is focusing on this going to make a difference
to your business?

_____

_____

_____

List all the key activities your business needs to do
to function:

_____

_____

_____

What are the key activities that raise awareness
about your products and helps increase sales?

_____

_____

_____

What do you love doing in your business?

_____

_____

_____

What tasks are important for you to do because you enjoy and perform them to an exceptional standard?

_____

_____

_____

What do you do in your business that only you can do?

_____

_____

_____

Look at your answers to questions 1 and 2. Do your team and systems support your goals?

_____

_____

_____

Do you need new systems or team members? If yes, what's required?

_____

_____

_____

Map it!

Now bring it all together. Look at your Map and cast your eyes over your Vision and Mission Statements. Refer to your answers above. You should be clear on the area you'll be focussing on. It is not only an area that you love and that only you can do, but your Zone of Genius should be something where you lose all sense of time, because you truly can't get enough of it.

If you're stuck doing tasks that you don't enjoy, start planning how you can delegate, automate or outsources. This is **your** business. Take action to focus on the areas that bring you joy! And know that this could be removing yourself from the business **completely**!

On your sticky note, add a line or two that summarises your Zone of Genius.

Day 7

Nurture Your Support System

"What I learn from talking to so many women around the world: If you can empower them with the right things, the right tools, they can lift up their family. And that ultimately lifts up their community and their society." ~ Melinda Gates, Philanthropist

Key Resources

Just like a car needs fuel, your business needs resources. The extent to which you know what resources you have access to at any given time within your business will help you plan for future events, help you feel excited knowing that you are ready for growth instead of panicked by an influx of business, and know that you're ready to take on the good, the bad and the ugly from a calm and collected place.

Neglecting yourself is not an option for you anymore. You must be clear on the people on your team (human resources), the money you have access to invest (financial resources), the coaches, mentors and communities you're connected with (emotional resources) and the physical resources you have that will help you make it happen. You'll also notice I include something a little different in there. Self-care. Yes, you are a resource too. Without you, none of this happens. Taking the time to look at what resources you currently have and what you may need will help you prepare for tomorrow.

Take note of the resources that might apply to you.

Physical Assets

This could be assets like a computer, a building or a warehouse. If your business is a manufacturing business or supermarket, these are great examples of businesses leaning on physical assets for resources. They know they need a space to sell their products, so they are more likely to acquire buildings or property and hold that as an asset.

Renting is an option, of course, and companies have various arrangements, depending on how that business will or will not impact the community for example, if a new part of a city is being developed (new houses are being developed) as a way to encourage people to purchase properties, retailers, supermarkets and now coffee shops are given incentives to rent properties at a lower cost as their presence can be attractive to home owners.

Intellectual Property

Intellectual property could include your patent, trademarks, copyright, anything that helps the public identify you as a brand.

Businesses that lean on intellectual property as a resource could be brands like Disney, sports brands like Nike and Adidas, and so on. These companies offer their name to many different products and services, some of which may not be created by them. These are called licensing agreements and can be how companies make their money.

Another example of a business that relies on having intellectual property as a key resource would be the music industry, where musicians write songs and earn royalties from their music being sold or performed.

Do you have intellectual property as a resource in your business? Consider your songs, your art, your designs, your photography, your databases, your tools, your systems or apps...

Humans

Having humans as a key resource is not necessary, nor indeed the main focus, for businesses these days.

An organisation that relies heavily on humans as a resource would be the Army. Armies need more humans entering the organisation to keep the system churning. During careers days at schools in UK, you may see the Army recruiting, because joining the Army is no longer compulsory. They know that people are the main resource of their business, so they need to get fresh people in.

Many businesses need humans to help them function efficiently. Whether you need staff or virtual assistants, understand how you will recruit loyal members into your team, what you will offer them and how you will be a valuable company to work for.

Finance

Finance can be used as a key resource for businesses, such as using credit as a way to get ahead of the competition. This strategy is used a lot in tech businesses, which borrow money heavily to beat their competitors to launch. This is why some companies may have millions invested in them before launching anything.

Businesses that use finance may be trying to stay ahead of the curve, whether by investing in new technologies or innovation, however any entrepreneur may use finance as a resource simply to ensure they're able to sufficiently operate their business and promote themselves through the start-up phases into securing business. This could mean using finance to get first pieces of equipment, for first runs of stock (if you have a product business that has upfront costs), as well as money to help the business flow.

Self-care

Making sure that you are well looked after enables you to do everything you need to do in your business. Without this, you won't function for long!

Making sure you eat well, taking care of your body through exercise, choosing food and drinks that nourish and replenish you, and getting adequate rest is important, since it's impossible to give your best when you're running on an empty battery.

Do you have time in your routine to relax and explore the beauty of the world around you? Self-care includes finding opportunities for joy and experiences you love that help you unplug from work, even for a few minutes each day, allowing the mind to rest. It's so easy to go from idea to idea, especially when you love what you do, but you must be intentional about taking a break! This could mean being out in nature, developing a meditation practice, reading books or poems, or listening to audio books or podcasts that make you smile. Do it in a way that works for you.

Self-care also means understanding who you are, what you need and being unapologetic about ensuring these needs are met, because if you're not blooming, it's more than likely that your business isn't either.

A coffee shop's key resources

Physical Assets

The location of a coffee shop chain is key and a resource for the company. A strategic placement of a coffee shop, for example, might be outside a train station. Located there, it will make much more money from travellers than another coffee shop 10 minutes down the road. Some coffee shop chains even own properties in key locations in all major cities, since it is such an important resource.

Intellectual Property

With many coffee shop chains creating branded merchandise, their trademarks are a valuable resource. Not only for driving footfall back to the stores (when people see others walking around with a branded coffee cup), but also as a part of selling product away from the fixed coffee shop location. We now see coffee shops selling their products through other retailers and licensing their brands in a similar way to Disney for example, I have seen a popular coffee shop chain's branding on plastic cups and bags being sold in a clothing store.

Humans

Having a constant supply of staff is important to a coffee shop chain, given that most cafe workers are people looking for flexible work, such as students. This is the ultimate key resource for a coffee shop, since business hinges around a customer being able to get a cup of coffee made for them.

It's important for a coffee shop chain to have incentives for staff to work with them, and to be transparent about how they treat them and pay them. Incentives could include fun days, spa days, whereas benefits could include a whole host of appealing schemes, from sick pay, to discounts with local businesses, concert venues, mobile phone contracts, insurance.

When deciding how to treat your staff, choose anything that makes their lives easier and more enjoyable.

Finance

Money can be used as a resource for a coffee shop chain, if the company leverages its access to finance and uses it to invest in new ideas before profits have been made. Many companies do this when they are looking to scale-up, but don't yet have access to funds of their own. This strategy can be risky so it's important to consult with a financial advisor before using finance in this way.

Self-care

The owner of the coffee shop chain may ensure they allocate enough breaks throughout the year in order to recharge and return to the company refreshed with a new perspective. It's common for small companies, chains and large corporations to allocate money towards retreats or personal development weekends set aside for senior members of staff like managers and executives.

If this is not the case, seeking support from a business coach, bringing a masseuse into your environment for your team's benefit or having additional people to support you at home are all options for the self-care and wellbeing of you and your people.

Not sure where to start? How about hiring a cleaner to ensure you have a relaxing environment when you return home from work?

How are you nurturing your support system?

Set your timer for 10 minutes and find out how you're doing and where you could improve the way you nurture your support system.

Complete the answers below then use the information to add sticky notes to the 'Support System' box of your Map.

Your Support System

Everything and everyone in your business needs TLC. Never take yourself, your people or your tools for granted. Look after your support systems and they'll be good to you!

Reflect on the last chapter and think about your key people. Include yourself if you work within your business. Who are your key human resources and what are your key tools or other resources that your business currently relies on or could lean on?

What do the people in your business need in order to thrive? (Encouragement, praise, support.)

_____

_____

_____

What tools do you need to support your goals? (Upgrades, updates, maintenance.)

_____

_____

_____

Map it!

Sticky note time. Add your key people and main resources, along with any ideas that came to mind to help support your business to thrive!

Day 8

Inspiring Strategies for Collaboration

"Collaboration has no hierarchy. The sun collaborates with soil to bring flowers on the earth." ~ Amit Ray, Author and Spiritual Teacher

Each block on the Creative Business Model Map provides a new opportunity for you to inject more creativity into your business. It's a chance to play and explore ideas, concepts that you may not have had fun with before. Collaborations and partnerships can be so exciting, because when done well, they allow you to serve and reach more people. They allow you to provide more to your existing network and can help position a new brand as an authority or even breathe life into an old business. They can also make or save you lots of money!

Exploring the world of partnerships and collaboration can make your business' plans come together! There is so much potential and exciting ways to form relationships. If you need more support in finding out what's possible for your brand, let's connect over at www.tracydurrant.com

Key Partnerships or Collaborations

So, how can partnerships benefit your business? Have you thought about what a key collaboration could offer? Before answer, first let's explore people's motivations for forming partnerships.

Economies of scale

[definition]

"The reduction of production costs that is a result of making and selling goods in large quantities, for example, the ability to buy large amounts of materials at reduced prices."
(Cambridge Dictionary)

An example of how 'economies of scale' could help a manufacturing business might be a food product partnering with a local farmer. Let's say you produce drinks and have the opportunity to buy the apples at a reduced cost if you purchase more apples. This could help you save money across a larger production run, helping you reduce the cost per drink unit meaning you'd make more profit. Using Economies of scale also help reduce costs for the farmer as selling more product to one client means they save time and money used when seeking new business and managing clients (general admin costs, invoicing and general client management) This can also help the farmer reduce wasting products which could cost them time and money in disposal costs (also helping the environment). This allows all parties to have a competitive edge.

This is an example of how optimising economy of scale can help your business. Can you think of any examples in your industry?

Reduce risk and uncertainty

Let's say you have a fitness watch prototype, one that monitors how many steps you take, and can provide you with data and updates to help you live a happy healthy life. But you don't have thousands to invest into marketing and your tech brand is new with no track record. What do you do?

To help reduce risk and uncertainty from the perspective of a buyer, you could partner with a business that's well-known in the fitness field, a known clothing brand, or an accredited technology company that will help strengthen the trust between you and your potential customers.

This is one way that having a strategic partnership can help people say 'yes' to purchasing from you, even if you are entering an unknown market.

Acquisition of resources and activities

Imagine you're in the mobile phone industry. You might have a company that designs beautiful phones that focuses on the design, colour and functionality of the phones, and knows how to attract the masses. However, your company may know little about the software needed to get this phone to work. This is where partnering comes in. Such a mobile phone business would partner with someone who could develop the technology to ensure the phone would be useful.

Wider audience

Joint ventures could provide opportunities for you to trade services in exchange for access to another person's audience. An example of this could be sharing valuable information with an organisation in exchange for being in a position of influence.

These are but a few of the motives you may have for forming partnerships.

Coffee shop collaborations

Let's come back to our coffee shop example and see how collaboration and partnership fits in.

Partnering with the producer

Coffee shop chains could partner with coffee farmers. It would make a difference if the coffee shop found a farm in keeping with their brand values and that reflects what's important to their customers. This would usually include a social focus, either giving back to the coffee farm community, ensuring trade is fair, and so on.

Custom-made coffee machines

A coffee shop chain is likely to have custom made machines. Partnering with a company that makes and can maintain the machines would be a prudent strategic partnership. This could be great for both parties, because the coffee machine maker gets consistent repeat business, while the coffee shop gets smaller upfront costs to purchase machines.

Perfect partnering

Usually, a partnership is non-competitive, so that both members bring different skills and assets to the table. For example, if you were a performer, you may want to partner with a company that produces microphones. See how these businesses have no crossover and equals a win-win.

What kind of key partnership could be good for your business?

(Hint hint! Refer to your Map and remind yourself of your values, vision and mission. Could key partnerships include collaborating with a social cause that you are passionate about? Can you align collaborative activities with your current goals?)

Set your timer for 10 minutes and dream up some inspiring collaborations by answering the questions below:

Inspiring collaborations

Take a look at your customer groups. Who could you collaborate with to enhance their experience?

_____

_____

_____

What brands would you love to collaborate with?

I'd love to partner/collab with	Ideas	How this benefits us both

Map it!

Make a decision to explore at least 3 ideas for collaborations, write it on your post it note and add it to the 'Collaborations' section.

Now set a date in your calendar for when you will reach out to that person or brand! You've just completed Day 8, you're amazing, you can make anything happen!

Day 9

Easy and Organised Cost Structures

"Successful people understand that you don't need to make things complicated." ~ Anne McKevitt, Entrepreneur, TV Personality, Author and Philanthropist

Typically, costs structures are the part that many don't enjoy, but we're going to make them easy and fun for your business! This is where you'll see if you have a profitable business opportunity or not. It's pretty important! Even if you'd rather outsource this task to someone else, you have to understand exactly what costs keep your business moving forward on a monthly basis.

I've lost count of the number of business owners I've met who have no idea what's going out of their account each month. Why aren't they looking at it? Money can bring up anxiety for so many of us, whether that looks like fears around spending and investing, fears that the money won't return, fears that it will be wasted. No matter your level of financial literacy, it's likely you'll have some money blocks. You're not alone in this and there are many resources that can help you move through them. For now, let's simply acknowledge that those concerns exist, take a breath and face the numbers.

Getting to grips with this will help you serve your customers with confidence. You deserve a profitable business. And making a profit starts with understanding, and maybe even enjoying, the numbers.

Costs

What are the most important costs within your business? Where will you source your products? What services will you need to pay for to help you run the business and serve your customers? Whether you're running a service-based business, product or coaching service, you'll have a combination of start-up costs, fixed costs and variable costs. And you'll have to take into account where money comes in and goes out of your business over time to ensure you have good cashflow.

Cash Flow Forecast

Forecasting when money will come in and out will help you understand if you are going to need a cash injection or need to remove certain costs to make sure you can pay for everything. Having a cash flow forecast, you'll be able to see where you can reduce costs. What kinds of costs might crop up? Let's take a look.

Start-up costs

These are one-off costs associated with getting your business from idea to launch. This could include research costs as well as pre-launch costs.

Fixed costs

Your fixed costs are the costs that stay the same, month by month, no matter how business is going. They include rent, utilities, salaries. They could also include software tools, your mailing list service, scheduling tools or website fees.

See below for a fuller list of potential fixed costs to consider:

- Payroll
- Marketing
- Premises
- Web hosting
- Phone
- Insurance
- Equipment
- Employee happiness/wellbeing
- Training
- Transport
- Professional fees
- Lawyer
- Entertainment/dinners and drinks
- Web development
- Branding/design
- Stationery

Variable costs

Also called direct costs, variable costs are those that go up or down, depending on the volume of sales. For you, what costs move depending on how much business you have? What are the costs directly related to you creating your products or services? How much labour time do you need to put in until you make a sale? How much do you need to spend on materials per item you sell?

For example, let's say you make and sell crystal necklaces. Your direct costs would be the time for making (labour) plus the chain, clasp and crystal materials plus packaging.

If you were a coach, variable costs could be how much advertising investment you need before it converts to a sale.

Economy of scale

Economy of scale is a situation where a business can get a financial advantage from bulk buying or paying in advance. For example, if you could purchase 100 items at $3 each or 1000 at $1 each, you make a financial gain by purchasing at the cheaper rate.

The drawback to the approach of purchasing more stock could be having higher upfront costs and needing to hold stock.

Another example of that is where you can make a saving on purchasing a year's subscription for a software package instead of paying a slight premium when you pay monthly.

The drawback to purchasing software for the year instead of per month could be the cost as well as you may find a new service that works better for you and don't want to find yourself paying for two services.

Are there any areas where your business could take advantage of economies of scale?

Cost structures for a coffee shop

Fixed costs

Possible fixed costs of a coffee shop include rent or mortgage, renting coffee machines, marketing (a fixed marketing budget), systems, staff and insurance.

Variable costs

Coffee/raw materials. There may be certain times of the year where they sell more or less of certain products.

Basic Finance Review

It's time for a quick review. Treat this task as a way of giving your business finances a basic review, rather than a comprehensive exercise, then work with a financial advisor or take the time to deep dive into this area in more detail. For the purpose of completing your Creative Business Model Map, I'd like you to consider your costs in a general sense, so you can get a feel for the numbers. In other words, I want you to be able to glance up at your Map and see what you're spending on marketing, staff, tax, utilities, tools etc.

Set your timer for 20 minutes and let's get clear on your cost structures!

(If you feel like you need more time or simply don't have this information, make note of the areas where you require help and set a date for locating this information. Do what you can right now.)

Cost Structures

Start-up costs:

_____

_____

_____

Fixed costs:

_____

_____

_____

Variable costs:

_____

_____

_____

Price of the products or services you sell:

_____

_____

_____

How many of these will you need to sell each month to reach your sales targets?

_____

_____

_____

What will be the cost of each sale?

_____

_____

_____

How many will you need to sell until you break-even?

_____

_____

_____

Map it!

Transfer this info onto your Map by writing your main metrics onto sticky notes.

Day 10

Unleash Exciting New Revenue Streams

"I love to see a young girl go out and grab the world by the lapels. Life's a bitch. You've got to go out and kick ass."

~ Maya Angelou, Author and Poet

There are so many ways to bring money into your business and life. Technology has made it so simple. In this chapter, we'll look at the opportunities currently available and sprinkle some creativity to get more money circulating!

Relying on only one stream of business income is not only risky, but it would mean not benefiting from the numerous ways that abundance can flow in. Who doesn't want to wake up to PayPal notifications from someone who bought your downloadable workbook while you were sleeping? Not only has the internet opened windows of opportunity to serve and share, but also there are countless ways to profit from your gifts in your local community.

Looking at how money already flows into your business (or the places you see money entering) then mind-mapping new ways you could exchange your skills, knowledge, expertise, services and products to serve your customer groups should be a fun and creative process. Then you'll balance this explorative task with what would feel amazing to you.

There may be money-making methods that you've overlooked. Perhaps you need fresh eyes on those concepts. Let's do that now and have fun looking at all the ways money can pour into your bank account... Dive into revenue streams and venture through the various ideas to tap into that money flow.

What Are Revenue Streams?

Revenue streams are the different services or products you could offer to your customers or clients and how much money you make from them. Here are six revenue stream ideas for any business.

Physical Products

Could you provide your customers with a workbook, pen, planner, t-shirt, bag, something that will complement your current products or services? Do you have a product to sell? Would you like to sell products in the future?

Subscriptions

Could you offer a subscription service or product? Most of us have signed up to a monthly subscription before, whether at the gym, membership to gain access to music or films. With subscriptions, your customers pay a monthly, quarterly or annual amount. Do you have a subscription service or product that you could offer?

Usage fee

Well known for utilities like telephones, electricity, gas and internet companies, you charge based on how much of a service has been used. If you use a cloud service to save your documents such as Dropbox or Google Drive you may pay a fee for how much storage space you use up on their servers.

Do you have a product or service where you could charge a usage fee? Is there a creative way that your business could use a usage fee?

Lending, renting and leasing

Trending lately, you may create a business where you allow your customers to lend, rent or lease products or services.

Rent the Runway, for example, has popular designer items on loan. They know people want more options for their wardrobe than their budget can handle, and don't want to be tied down with items of clothing that they'll never wear again and will take up space they don't have.

Other popular businesses make revenue through leasing other people's property, such as would-be car hire company Zipcar where people can loan their cars, or home rental like Airbnb.

Licensing

Another way you could bring money into your business is through licensing, giving people the rights to use your brand name, your logo, or something else where you own the intellectual property.

It could be licensing music, the use of your artwork or designs. You could licence your work in different industries for different countries for different lengths of time.

Sometimes you could receive a flat fee, sometimes you could receive a percentage.

Courses

A great way to bring additional money into your business is by teaching your audience. You could share an element of your personal service by way of a course.

Let's say you're a stylist. You might put together a course to help creative entrepreneurial women build their capsule wardrobe. This could be taught digitally, in-person via workshops, through workbooks, books, audiobooks or seminars.

Could you teach an element of your service? Is there a workshop waiting to be unleashed by your brand?

Those are just six ways you could generate revenue in your business, but there are many more. Find more examples at www.tracydurrant.com/planitnowbook

Potential revenue streams for a coffee shop

This list explores ideas for our case study coffee shop.

- Product sales
- Physical assets
- Signature coffee cups
- Coffee mugs at retail stores
- Tumblers
- Franchising as a revenue stream

- Selling instant coffee into supermarkets
- Product sales through an online store
- Coffee design workshops

As you can see, there are many different ways a coffee shop chain could bring revenue into their business other than their core business of making coffee. Did any of the above ideas spark ideas for you?

Why have just one way to bring money into your business when you can have many? Let's identify three areas where you're currently bringing money into your business, how much money is flowing in and how much you'd like to see within the next 6 to 12 months. (I suggest doing this kind of planning at least twice a year.) What exciting ways can you welcome new money into your business? Let's increase your capacity for circulating money!

Set your timer for 20 minutes and discover what exciting ways you'll bring income in:

Revenue Streams

My business is currently bringing in _____ per month

I'd like to increase that to about _____ per month

Add those numbers to your Map.

List the revenue streams through which your business currently brings money.

_____

_____

_____

Are there any additional revenue streams that you'd like to add? If so, what will they be? (Add these to a sticky note for your Map.)

_____

_____

_____

Map it!

Once you've completed your answers, use the information to add sticky notes to the tenth and final block, 'Revenue Streams'.

You're All Done!

That's it! You're done! You planned it now... in just 10 days.

I hope the tools, worksheets and methods you have explored over the last 10 days have helped you see how doable business can be and helped you quit your burnout business (even avoid one completely if this is your first business). You are on your way to creating a business and life that puts your dreams and desires front and centre.

At the beginning of this book, I mentioned how I experienced burnout and struggled to find balance between my business and personal life. I want you to understand that it's possible for you to create that balance. It's so important for the health of your business, the quality of your life, and your mental and physical state.

Sharing this message of growth, abundance and balance changed the way I do business and life. Women wanting to be, do and have it all, but still putting their own personal wellbeing on the backburner has to stop.

It's time to stay connected with your vision and be unapologetic with your self-care. Get the support you desire, listen to the breaks your body cries out for, rest and use the resources that will make it easier to live in flow.

I used to think that being successful meant finding out and teasing out every possible detail, going to every workshop and reading every book on the shelf so I was prepared. Now I understand that the information I need will find me. However you connected with the methods in this book, I hope it serves you in gaining perspective so you can create the impact in the world that you've always desired to make.

The more I grow, the more I want to share what I've learned along the way. I believe knowledge is great, but sharing that with others so they can have breakthroughs and extend their creativity further is one of the reasons I love to support business owners with resources, workshops and one-to-one coaching.

From the work you put in over the last 10 days, you should now be:

1. Clearer about what you want from your business

2. Passionate and strong on the vision you have for your business and life
3. Energised and motivated to transform those easy-to-access ideas on your Map into reality
4. Excited about your future and the future of your business
5. Able to clearly identify how to implement the information from the 10 building blocks
6. Experiencing more growth and profits while using less energy
7. Focused on your own Zone of Genius.

If you're ready to take the next step from having a clear Creative Business Model Map to executing what you've learned through additional support to help you create transformational results, let's connect over on www.tracydurrant.com.

You now have a simple method for turning your ideas from concept to something workable. Hopefully, you find this method fun and can make it part of your yearly, quarterly or monthly practice to see what's working in your business and what needs creative attention.

Share this book to ward others off a burnout business. Let them know there's another way to grow their business. Go out there and continue to share your gifts with the world, because in doing so, you create economic freedom for all.

Keep creating and inspiring,

Tracy xx

Mission and Vision:

Date:

Customer Groups	Aligning with customers	Creating Real Connections	Support System
		Delivery	Collaborations
		Zone of Genius	
Simple Cost Structures		Exciting Revenue Streams	

Download and print your Creative Business Model Map.

Go to www.tracydurrant.com/mymap

About the Author

"You are an Artist. You are a Creative. It's your mission to share your truth. Something magic happens when you do."

My name is Tracy Durrant and I'm an intuitive business and lifestyle coach. I help creative entrepreneurs make a consistent income from their gifts.

Why? Because I want you to know that it's safe to explore your passions. You can make money doing what you love.

I know it might seem difficult at times. I've been there. I've burned out before. But I quit my burnout business and purposely launched my dream business. Now I do what I love, while helping others do the same.

Entrepreneurship has always been a spiritual journey for me. Seeing your ideas through to completion has a ripple effect that positively transforms your life and those around you. It strengthens my belief that we're all on this planet to expand, love and share.

I have over six years of experience coaching clients one-to-one. I want to help support your business and life goals, so you feel confident,

connected and supported. That is my goal, whether you're working with me one-to-one or whether you're on one of my digital courses.

Want to know more? Go to my website and arrange a chat. I'm here to help.

www.tracydurrant.com

With Gratitude

Thank-you to my family & friends who have supported me on my journey.

My business coaches & mentors, past and present.

The Authors & Creatives who continue to inspire me.

So many people have helped me in this process and I appreciate you all.

References

Content in this book has been inspired by 'Business Model Generation: A Handbook for Visionaries, Game Changers, and Challengers' (Alexander Osterwalder and Yves Pigneur, 2010) & The Business Model Canvas (Alexander Osterwalder, 2008.)

Day 6 (Zone of Genius)

The Big Leap: Conquer Your Hidden Fear and Take

Life to the Next Level (Gay Hendric, 2010)